# What Can I Say?

words by:

# WendiSue

Bluegrass PUBLISHING

www.theultimateword.com

270 · 251 · 3600

**For information write:**
Bluegrass Publishing, Inc.
PO Box 634
Mayfield, KY 42066 USA
service@theultimateword.com
www.BluegrassPublishing.com


ISBN: 0-9761925-0-0

1st Edition
Mayfield, KY : Bluegrass Publishing, Inc, 2005


Proudly printed in the United States of America

First Edition © 2005

# Table of Contents

Have you ever put together the perfect scrapbook page, but couldn't find the perfect words to express the thoughts and feelings of that day? The written word can have the power to touch hearts, inspire minds, and even give light to our souls.

"What can I say?" contains Over 100, newly created, original poems and expressions that are as varied as your scrapbook pages! This is not merely a book of quotes or one-liners, but rather a unique collection designed to complete your perfect page.

The creators of "What can I say?" have, for years, been asked to write poetry and prose for family and friends. The spectrum has been vast. Our written expressions have found their way to birthdays, anniversaries, baptisms, memorials, announcements, gift tags, cards, stationery, bookmarks, speeches... Oh! And of course, SCRAPBOOKS! We are sure that you can think of thousands of uses of your own. Everyday life has not only been the purpose of our writing, but the fulfillment of it as well. We know that the "write" expressions can turn an ordinary page into an EXTRAORDINARY one!

This book is simple to use. Copy the poem you want directly to your paper, cut, then paste to your scrapbook page. In addition to adding important names and dates, you will find that it will enhance your journaling.

Remember, Your pictures are worth a thousand words...and what you say about them will be PRICELESS!

We hope that you, as well, will find the fulfillment, not only in everyday life, but in making everyday a legacy of your own.

"Write" from our heart to yours,

Wendi Sue

Spring has sprung!
A new season's begun.
Sunshine and smiles for everyone!

SPRING is here!
The world is singing!
The earth is full of Wonderful things!

Sun, sun summertime...
Fun, Fun all the time...
We're together and all is fine...
We SMILE all in the Summertime!

# SNOW
is falling all around

On my nose and
on the ground!

I love to **play**
all day in snow.

Until my toesies
get too **cold**!

Autumn leaves fall all around
from the treetops
to
the
ground...
**colors bright**
for me to see,
Leaves are falling down on me.

Autumn colors warm my soul

Aglow with brown and red and gold.

Lights in our lives are the amber hues,

Recalling sweet memories to our view.

STARLIGHT STARBRIGHT
Keep our snowman here tonight so when we wake up we can play with our new friend just one more day!

# Angels

Wherever you go...
Whatever you do...
May Angels always
Watch over you.

Angels are watching us from above,
They follow our path
And they wrap us in love.
Whenever you feel the warmth around you,
You'll know that your angel
Is watching you too!

Tiny Angel baby
Filled with heaven's light
A new little shining star
Our family's sweet delight.

# Angel Friends

There are many kinds of friends around,
Some old, some new, some still to be found.
But the best kind of friend to have at your side,
Whenever you feel that you need a guide,
Is an Angel friend...sent from above,
To share with you some of God's great love.

An Angel friend is always there,
Willing to love and willing to care,
Ready to help with your heavy load
Ready to guide you down the right road.

God didn't send us to earth all alone,
He tied us together in a plan of his own.
Angel friends play a special part,
They're the string that connects us...
From heart to heart.

So the next time you're looking for a friend to be true,
Remember there's an Angel friend...
Waiting for you.
And after you've felt the friendship shared,
Then share it with others and
Show that you care!

# Announcing

**BABIES...**
are proof of God's existence.

A baby GIRL
Oh, what a pearl!

**A baby BOY**
**Oh, what a joy!**

**5** little
**fingers**

**5** little
**toes**

Pretty blue eyes
and a button nose
A baby as sweet
as heaven could be
THANKS, GOD
For sending this angel to me!

We've been blessed
with a new little boy
He fills our lives
with love and joy!

Welcome little one, so dear,
We're happy now that you are here.
We've waited long for you to come,
Now your sweet life has just begun.

Our little ray of sunshine
Has come from up above
To brighten up our life and home
And share with us God's love.

A sweet angel
We dearly love
Was sent to us
From heaven above.

sweet little baby face

Innocent and bright,
Shines from within
like a glowing ray of light.

Sent down from heaven
To bless us from above,
A shining star straight from the sky
to fill our home with love.

Original Expressions Wendi Sue

# As I Grow

LOOK
I'm BIG.
I'm GROWING fast.
Enjoy me now . . .
MY SIZE WON'T LAST!

RIDING MY BIKE
IS REALLY A TRICK
BUT I HAVE TO BE CAREFUL...
THE SIDEWALK IS SLICK!

Sure!
It was fun
To swivel about,
But my hair's being cut
So now
I want out!!

EXPLORING
Is what I like to do.
It's always FUN
To find something new!

I'm as #*icky as can be ... 'cause I can ride a bike you see!

EVERY FLOWER IS DIFFERENT
AND SO IS EVERY CHILD
ALTHOUGH THEY'RE FROM THE SAME SEED,
SOME GROW A BIT MORE WILD!
BUT EACH ONE CAN BE SPECIAL
IF THEY'RE ALLOWED TO BLOOM
SO TEND THEM WHILE THEY'RE GROWING
BUT GIVE THEM LOTS OF ROOM.

My angry words spoken
showed hurt in her eyes.
But small tender arms
proved SHE was most wise.
"Mommy, I love you,"
she said with regret.
Now, what had she done?
I simply forget!

*Original Expressions Wendi Sue*

"Mommy, hold me,"
she said to me.
"Not right yet,
I'm busy you see."

A tear on her cheek...
The wavering voice...
Told me for certain
I'd made the wrong choice.

So,

Into my arms
I scooped her up tight.
Today was the day
I'd set all things right.

I'd spend time with her,
My Darling ... My Own.
I know I can't wait,
For then she'd be grown.

Little wobble walker
Just learning how to go.

Up and down and all around
And leaning to and fro'.

We must enjoy the moment,
'cause before you even know

This little wobble walker
Will be running with the show.

Food on my cheeks
Food in my hair
MY FOOD...
GOES just about everywhere!
But even though I'm a messy me,
I'm still...
as cute as I can be!

Years will come ... and years will go
But NEVER
do they seem so slow...
As when our baby's toddling!

Original Expressions Wendi Sue

# Birthday Wishes

Happy Birthday Little One
Your happy days have just begun!
We're so glad you're part
Of our dear family
Here's hoping that your birthday
Is happy as can be!

Ice Cream and Birthday Cakes
are **messy** as can be
But once a year a mess is fine
This party's just for **me**!

**B**irthdays
are so very **F**un!
It's MY day
I'm **#1**

My birthday fun
has just begun
today I'm big
I'm turning ONE!

A birthday wish!
Can you guess who?
It's MY day
I'm turning TWO!

I am happy
as can be...
'cause today
I'm turning THREE!

Wishing candles,
kisses and more,
TODAY this KID
is turning FOUR!

 Wishing candles,
kisses and more,
TODAY this BOY
is turning FOUR!

 It's a birthday
a birthday surprise
Now look
look who's FIVE!

 Birthdays are
the biggest kicks...
Especially when
you're turning SIX!

 Who's been sent
to us from HEAVEN?
Look, it's ME
I'm turning SEVEN!

 Today is GREAT...
I'm turning EIGHT!

 It's my day
to sing and shine,
because today
I'm turning NINE!

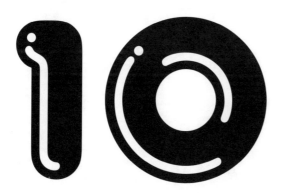 Birthday time
is here again,
I'm so glad
I'm turning TEN!

# Boys Will be Boys

Cars    Trucks    Trains    and    Toys

## Happiness is ... Little boys!

### LITTLE BOY BLUE

WITH A TWINKLE IN HIS EYE

IS DADDY'S LITTLE HELPER

AND MOMMY'S CUTIE PIE!

Cowboy Joe
Ready to go
All dressed up
For the big Rodeo!

## OVERALLS

with worn out knees...
Boys like mud puddles
and climbing trees.

Original Expressions Wendi Sue

# Christmas Cheer

HOLIDAY MEMORIES
Warm the soul,
Strengthen the spirit,
Lighten the burden,
And bless the day
Of friends and family who share

The best kind of Christmas
Comes from the heart
With family and friends
All doing their part
To share with each other
The love and the light
We received from the gift
On that first Christmas night.

We gather around
the Christmas tree
With grateful hearts
and thoughts of Thee.

*Family traditions*
*and friends so dear*
*Bless us at Christmas*
*and all through the year!*

**Having friends and family near**
**Makes the best kind of Holiday Cheer.**

WISE MEN SEEK HIM STILL
WITH GIFT OF HEART TO GIVE.
IF WE WOULD BUT DO HIS WILL
ETERNALLY WE'LL LIVE.

May your mittens warm your fingers
May hot chocolate warm your soul
May the spirit of the season
Fill your heart with heaven's glow!

## The Candy Cane

The Candy Cane's a treat for the Christmas season
But it's not just to eat...there's a much greater reason.

The cane symbolizes a shepherd's crook
Of a shepherd so loving and kind
Who looks after His sheep, keeping care of them all
So not one should be left behind.
The color of white is the pure of His soul
Left unspotted by all of the world.
The red is the sacrifice He freely gave
So we'd always be part of His fold.

Who is He you ask?
Turn your cane upside down
And you'll see the first sign of His name.
Don't forget Him this year,
He shared His great love
And He's hoping
we'll all do the same.

Help us
remember
in doing
our part
to love
one another
and give
from the heart.

As the Christmas Season gets here
And you find you're in a hurry
With baking, shopping, decorating . . .
And things that make you worry,
Stop a while, and take some time
To think about the season.

And why we do all that we do . . .
What really is the reason?

Take some time to build a snowman
And enjoy the winter air
Share a smile with a child,
Let your neighbors know you care.

Fill your heart with love and joy
And spread it all around
Through the magic of a snowman,
A new joy you have found!

When the season's finally over
And your snowman melts away,
Keep the love inside your heart
And share some everyday.

For the magic of the snowman
Can last the whole year through,
If you can just remember . . . It's really up to you!

# Family Tree

Earth sends new life
The blooms of family,
And love gives root
To the branches on our tree.
And though some leaves may fall,
Our tree branches out again.
More lovely with the spring,
Because family has no end.
For all that we are,
For life and love and memory,
For people we adore,
We grow our family tree.

**FAMILY**

**Family traits and close-knit ties ever bind us through our lives.**

**So Together we meet as friends, thankful our heritage makes us kin.**

*Original Expressions Wendi Sue*

North

# HOME

*Is Where I Like The Best!*

West

East

*South*

My little baby brother

all his hurts I mend.

I dry his little tears,

for he's my special friend.

Of all the places on earth I know,
There's no where else I'd rather be
It's the place my heart loves best
It's the place called **FAMILY**.

Cousins are cute
Cousins are sweet
And cousins like playing
Whenever they meet.

My **precious** little **sister**
Is mine **throughout** the years.
I **kiss** her when she **cries**
and **wipe away** her tears.

*Perhaps we chose each other*
As a family here on earth,

*Destined to be stitched with love*
Before each mortal birth.

*Perhaps we had the chance there*
To choose another way

*But if the Choice was given now,*
**MY FAMILY** is where I'd stay.

# GRANDMAS GIVE THE GREATEST HUGS
# THEY MAKE YOU WARM INSIDE
# THERE'S JUST NOTHING LIKE A GRANDMA'S HUG...
# TO BRIGHTEN UP YOUR LIFE.

I love to sit on GRANDPA'S LAP
and listen to his stories…
of all the things he used to do,
when he was young like me.
And oh, what FUN on grandpa's lap,
when he can be a horsey,
he makes me laugh and swing about
a-bouncing on his knee.

# Forever Friends

## HEART to HEART FRIEND to FRIEND

May your life be blessed
Until we meet again.

**Best Buddies** are hard to find ...

I'm so glad

is a small thing to lend

A giving hand

It doesn't take courage

to be a good friend!

that you are mine!

I'll whisper in your ear

A secret from my heart.

The promise of true friends ...

Soul mates from the start.

Through the years we'll dream

Of all the days we spent

In the wonder of a whisper ...

And think of promises kept.

**Life's not always easy…**
I guess I know it's so.

**But there's always someone special**
To help when I'm feeling low.

**She's my friend, my sister, pal**
Who always knows just what to do.

**When I fall she picks me up,**
And to her word, she's ever true.

**I trust her with my secrets,**
And of her patience, there's no doubt.

**I love her, and she loves me…**
That's what friends are all about.

# BEST FRIENDS

We'll always be
side by side
just you and me!

If I had a second chance,

And I could choose again,

There's not a question in my mind,

I'd choose you for my friend.

I'd like to say we met by chance,
But that's not quite the truth.

Yet when we met, I felt as though
I'd known you since my youth.

Sisters by heart, friends by name
So many thoughts, we have just the same.

There for each other
Through thick and through thin,

It takes someone special
To call a true friend.

It was God's inspiration that brought us together,
And that's how I know We'll be friends forever.

# Happy Anniversary

In days gone by . . . .
I loved you so
To my heart you held the key
Though so many years
have passed
More precious now are you to me.

A time for us to celebrate

As years are passing by

You're still the one I love the most,

The sparkle of my eye!

## HAPPY ANNIVERSARY
To my darling one
Each day you make it seem
As though our love
has just begun.

# In the Garden

I'm a little squirt
Who likes to dig in the dirt
And work in the Garden too.
And someday I'll grow
Just like the weeds I hoe
So fast, you won't know what to do!

Working together, the garden grows

As the garden grows, the family knows
The labors of love and careful sowing

Are worth all the work,
When the garden is growing.

In the GARDEN
Seeds are planted.
Working together
HANDS united.
Garden's GROWING,
Hearts are knowing,
Good THINGS come...
From careful sowing.

# Memories

PICTURE BY PICTURE . . . PAGE BY PAGE

*Preserved for the future . . . and treasured today.*

## DAYDREAMS

I wander through stories yet to be told

As I treasure the dreams of a beautiful day.

And when hopes are fulfilled and I am old

I'll think back as I dream of my carefree play.

Tears of **Joy** And tears of **PAIN**

Tears coming down Like drops of rain!

Sunflower Dreamer

Memories captured are Memories made. of carefree days

# Outdoor Adventures

A walk in the park
on a nice sunny day
Makes worries and troubles
Fade away

GREAT RUSHING STREAMS

**CANYONS SO BROAD,**

FLOWERS FROM HEAVEN

**IN THE MOUNTAINS OF GOD.**

I love to go fishing and cast out my pole

Then reel in a big one from my fishing hole

I'll hold him up high with a SMILE to show

When it comes to fishin'
there's not much I don't know!

# WATERMELON

*in the sun*

# PICNIC TIME

*For everyone!*

1ˢᵗ, 2ⁿᵈ, 3ʳᵈ &

**BASEBALL** HOME

*season has begun!*

I love to go four
**WHEELIN'**
With the tires just a
**PEELIN'**
And the noise they make a
**SQUEALIN'**
Makes a heart just feel...
**A THRILLIN'**

Picnic Time for everyone!

*Picnics can be lots of fun.*

Eating, laughing, sharing smiles...

*Memories building all the while!*

# Swimming...
## like a fish at sea...
## when water gets all over me!

Bring your shovel ...
Bring your pail ...
We're going to the
# BEACH!
The water chases us around
And sand tickles our feet!

Camping under stars and trees,

Feeling of the mountain breeze.

Quiet, peaceful scenes of view,

I love camping out with you.

# Sandcastles to heaven!
## A starfish for thee.

## Oh! Leave me to
# DREAM
## By the glittering
## sea!

# Playtime!

In the park there's much to do...
I'll *swing*...
And *slide*...
And *smile* for you!

**PLAYING**
with my favorite toys...
brings me
lots of joy!

## Dress Up

A PRINCESS in her tower...

Sometimes a pretty flower.

A bird that soars throughout the sky,

A proper Lady, hand held high.

I'm a dancer in perfect step,

A CHEERLEADER with lots of pep...

But no matter the part I play,

it's always **ME** at the end of day!

*Original Expressions Wendi Sue*

Join with me in tea for two
I'll show you what you need to do.
Take a seat and hold the cup
I'll pour . . . then you drink it up!

KITTENS ARE PRECIOUS
THEY CUDDLE AND PURR...
THERE'S JUST NOTHING BETTER
THAN NICE COZY FUR!

Puppies are roly and poly and sweet
They chew on my nose
And they tickle my feet!

Me and my horse have a JOLLY old time.

We gallop and play...

He's a great FRIEND of mine!

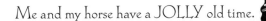

I feed him and brush him, then put him away,

So tomorrow we're rested...

And ready to PLAY!

# Red White and Blue

Our forebears saw in vision
The home our land would be.
They sought not for oppression
But instead, for LIBERTY.

Oh! How the brave paid with their tears!
So, as their gift is passed to you,
May it stand throughout the years
EVER BRIGHTER … EVER TRUE.

In harmony let us ever live
That tolerance and love abide …
Hope, Dear Country, that God may give
His greatest blessings from above.

AMERICA
stands proud
AMERICA
stands true
AMERICA
we love you

the red white and blue

America … Red White and Blue
My Country Free …
I do love you.
America … Red White and Blue
Thank You
For the freedom true!

# Remembrance

You sent him here to love …

I now return him to Your care.

Keep him, Heavenly Father

Waiting safely for me there.

May I always remember this child of mine,

Is also a child of one …

## More Divine

A child of God is a blessing you see

I'm so thankful He chose

to share this one with me.

### Sunset

We crossed the paths of life,

better for having done.

But now, from our view,

he is the setting sun.

Yet, what can I repay?

His memory tells me …

Yes, in tomorrow's sunrise

that I might live as he.

### Sunset

We crossed the paths of life,

better for having done.

But now, from our view,

she is the setting sun.

Yet, what can I repay?

Her memory tells me …

Yes, in tomorrow's sunrise

that I might live as she.

## A Child of God

You lived with Him there,
Then He gave you a Home
And parents who care.

May He watch you…

And guide you…

And send you His love.

May we always give thanks,
For His gift from above.

You sent her here to love …

I now return her to Your care.

Keep her, Heavenly Father

Waiting safely for me there.

*Original Expressions Wendi Sue*

# Schools and Rules

Dear Teacher,

You've given too much to repay.

Hopes for Tomorrow,

And Dreams for Today.

aBC's and 123's...
Preschool is so fun for me.
We smile and laugh
...and grow
...and sing
I learn to do so many things!

SCHOOL HaS started
and it's my first Day.
Mommy is sad 'cause I'm going away...

I told Her,
"DON'T WORRY,"
that I'll come back Home,

but sHe maybe won't know me
because I'll Have grown!

*Original Expressions Wendi Sue*

# Sugar and Spice

Little girls are quite a treat
All lace and curls,
Oh! How Sweet!

Dolls and dresses…
Ribbons and curls…
Happiness is…little Girls!

Girls are… Flowers,
Girls are… Pink…
Girls can make boys…
Forget how to think!

She's Daddy's Little Girl,
The sunshine in his day.
Bright hope for his tomorrow,
She's in his heart to stay!

The "Dancing Queen" just watch her go…
Be careful now, she'll steal the show!

# Sunshine and Smiles

You are my SUNSHINE ...
Bright as can be.

Each day I thank GOD
That He sent you to me!

Spread your smile all around
For smiles are like the sunshine

They're better UP than when
they're Down!

LIFE IS A PARTY,
A TIME TO CHEER
CELEBRATE MEMORIES ALL THROUGH THE YEAR!

*Original Expressions Wendi Sue*

With colors of Red, Yellow and Blue,
God sent this RAINBOW

# Especially for YOU!

**Butterflies**
*Flutter by*
in the sky
before my eyes

Their colors **BRIGHT**
Their **MESSAGE** clear
*they've come to tell me*
**GOD is NEAR**

Sunshine and Smiles

Brighten up the days

They warm...and cheer...

And gladden hearts

And shine along the way!

BE **KIND**
AND BE **GIVING**
BE **LOVING**
AND **TRUE**

WHEN YOU DO
THIS TO OTHERS,
THEY WILL DO IT
TO YOU!

*As pretty as a picture* ♡ *As soft as a rose* ♡ *As warm as the sunshine*

## Filled with Heaven's glow.

# Through the Year

Please be mine... *Oh Valentine!*
You're sweet as you can be.
I'll give you chocolate candy,
And a *Hug* and *Kiss* from me!

The STARS are out
It's the FOURTH OF JULY
Dozen's of FIREWORKS
LIGHT up the SKY!

The Easter Bunny comes each year
Bouncing through with Easter cheer.
We color our eggs,
then we play hide and seek...
Making Easter memories we'll always keep!

SPOOKS AND GOBLINS,
A FULL MOON TOO
ARE OUT TONIGHT
AND SURE TO SCARE YOU!

Original Expressions Wendi Sue

# Toddle Time

## The **WRITING** ON THE WALL

Is very plain to see,
But not so plain to read,

'cause it was done by **ME**!
(And I'm not even three!)

 Is where

I like to sleep

With blankets

nice and cozy.

I want to keep

We snuggle

nose to nosy.

Goodnight sweet little sleepy head,

*Sleep tight 'till morning's here,*

And when you wake...

Your mommy's arms
Will love and hold you near.

I'm so **big**
Just watch me **grow**
Each day I **grow**
From **head to toe**

Look at me...
...I'm messy as can be!
But I'm so glad
Mommy still loves me!

Roses Are Red
Violets Are Sweet

Without my TEDDY
I JUST CAN'T SLEEP!

Original Expressions Wendi Sue

Giggles and SMILES
and dimply cheeks.
Bright shiny eyes
and a laugh just as sweet.
For all these reasons
I love you and more.
You're my sweet baby
I'll always adore!

This baby of mine...

I know it won't last...

Before I know it,

You'll grow up too fast!

Splish...Splash...

...Splish...Splash

We LOVE a Bubble Bath

Baths and bubbles
make some fun,
splash around
on everyone

Scrub-a-dub-dub...
Look at me in the tub!

Original Expressions Wendi Sue

# Vows of Love

Two **HANDS** joined together
at the dawning of the sun
Our **LIVES** so intertwined
have only just begun…

For all our **DREAMS** begin anew
so that when each day is done
and throughout our lives together
our **HEARTS** will be as one.

## BOYS WILL BE BOYS AND PLAY WITH THEIR TOYS...

Girls will be Girls
and do up their curls. . .

Then one day soon …
the two hearts will meet,

And the rest of the story is … OH SO SWEET!

Endless are
our bands of
gold,
The circle
of our love we
hold.

Endless still...
will our love be
fron now until
Eternity.

I am yours
and you are mine
Together through the end of time.

Good and bad
will come and go
Yet through it all...

Our Love will grow.

My vows of love I give to you
a promise to be ever true

Your vow that you will always be
my soulmate through eternity

The vows of love we take tonight
forever more our hearts unite.

# The End?

Not Really...

Bluegrass Publishing is proud to share this wonderful beginning with Wendy and Bonnie. We extend our heartfelt thanks to both of these extraordinary women for allowing us to share their God-given gift of words with you.

## ...more books coming!

# More Books from the Ultimate Line...

**BLUEGRASS PUBLISHING, INC.**
## ORDER FORM

NAME | DATE

ADDRESS

CITY/STATE

CREDIT CARD # | EXP. DATE

PHONE ( ) —

E-MAIL

| QTY | TITLE | EACH | TOTAL |
|-----|-------|------|-------|
| | The Ultimate Guide to the Perfect Word<br>BY LINDA LATOURELLE • **OUR BIGGEST SELLER** | $19.95 | |
| | The Ultimate Guide to the Perfect Card<br>BY LINDA LATOURELLE • **NEW/BIGGER-384 PG** | $19.95 | |
| | The Ultimate Guide to Celebrating Kids I<br>BY LINDA LATOURELLE • **BIRTH TO PRESCHOOL** | $19.95 | |
| | The Ultimate Guide to Celebrating Kids II<br>BY LINDA LATOURELLE • **NEW/GRADE SCHOOL** | $19.95 | |
| | LoveLines—Beautifully designed quotes<br>BY LINDA LATOURELLE • **NEW/COPY & USE** | $12.95 | |
| | Where's Thena? I need a poem about...<br>BY THENA SMITH | $19.95 | |
| | Whispers: Passionate Poetry<br>BY THENA SMITH | $12.95 | |

SEND ORDER TO:

**BLUEGRASS PUBLISHING, INC**
PO BOX 634
MAYFIELD, KY 42066
**(270) 251-3600**
FAX (270) 251-3603

| | |
|--|--|
| 6% TAX KEN-TUCKY | |
| $2.95 Per Book | |
| **TOTAL AMOUNT** | |
| $ | |

## WWW.BLUEGRASSPUBLISHING.COM

# Thank You
## For your order

Bluegrass PUBLISHING

www.theultimateword.com

270·251·3600